Sentenced

Fil Deptula

BookLeaf Publishing

India | USA | UK

Presentation by *BookLeaf Publishing*

Web: www.bookleafpub.com

E-mail: info@bookleafpub.com

ISBN: 9789358314397

First edition 2023

to my wife, Christina

PREFACE

"Stranded is, indeed, the reverse of sinking."
Joseph Conrad - The Mirror of the Sea

The Sentencing of Malcolm Washington

On the day he was

                                  sentenced(.),

on the day he was told
how long it was meant by
– mandatory minimum –
on the day the slow

                    realization

seeped into him
like liquid lead filling lungs
constricting breath
like the smoke that helped caused this mess,
on the day he wished he lived
on the other side of arbitrary boundary,
and wished to be portrayed as
one of us, one as you,
on the day a mother
was carried out of the courtroom
by a brother
too hysterical to walk,
crying for her child as if
she had just lost him forever,
on the day he'd never seen
so many tears
tear up a family
on the day he walked through

that iron door
where he would
be forced
to call home,
now a criminal,
on the day he was stripped of his possessions,
stripped of his liberty,
on the day he reflected how
it was a routine stop,
that he swore he wasn't swerving
that it wasn't his,
that his friend honestly left it,
that there wasn't even a smell,
that they had no right to search him,
that the dog didn't need to be brought,
on the day he had found out that
his youth was over, that he would
be treated as an adult,
on the day that fear that had controlled it
began to calcify into contempt and resentment,
on the day he hugged his mother
and knew it might be the last time
he could as a free person,
he wore the only suit his owned,
the same suit
he bought second hand
for senior prom
six weeks prior.

Always Connected, All the Time

I grab my phone –
nothing –
place in my pocket,
but within moments
I nervously reach for it again,
forgetting the
disappointing interaction
I had seconds ago.
I go into my messages
to see if it's lying.
It's not.
I put it away
and then check it again.
Same.

It's September.
I'm sitting on a dock of a lake
on a late afternoon that will soon retire.
Somewhere, a lonely loon cries.
It keeps crying but there's no mate to be found.
I reason that's impossible:
loons aren't endangered.
I look back down at my phone,
still –
nothing.

Dédoublement

In her mind,
the other woman is not only a threat,
she's a dependent.

She's the branch with a solitary withered leaf
ready to collapse from years of repressing sunshine,
and the other is deluge,
the overabundance of a life-force that should
provide normalcy.

She is burnt out,
a feigned sigh of relief,
an engine running on fumes,
a battery out of juice.

She finds herself in a glass box
waiting for her troubles to finally break,
falling down in tiny, sharp droplets
forming puddles of mirrors below her feet
a reminder to look down at her reflection.

Unsure of who she is today,
which part of her
is staring back at her –
she opens herself to her own scrutiny,
revisits when it all went wrong,
of when she became Pandora.

The Philosopher

The philosopher sorts through clustered thought,
hiding the rest in the overcrowded
closet of his mind –
his thoughts a dancing daydream,
a gazpacho of metaphysical manifestations –
and concludes that "mom" is
the most beautiful palindrome,
and "dad"
a necessary evil.

He exists, he concludes,
as ragged form and haggard beard,
and fumbles through his torn jacket
to sort through the stockpile
of basic necessities
finally fishing out a crumpled receipt
and the solitary pen
to transcribe
his next prophecy,
signing the note
with oily fingers
as he always does.

He reigns over his domain
alone in Battery Park,

dependent on his followers' generosity, alone, and homeless.

Alement

It was suppose to be *itsneverjus*t one drink –
something to taper off
the rough Tuesday evening (dark clouds
sweep over moonless sky) –
because all day *coldsweetbrowneffervesce*
the desire Need is
resisted to let everything go (first
thunder), to let *whyshouldnti* inhibition
lay fallow, let work
maybeonemoremaybeonemorelastonedidntquitedoit (hard
rain
commences) go undone, for there always
onemore (in the distance, lightning) tomorrow,
and after the *onetwothrefourfiveemptied* years
of commitment (wind splashes rain
against a tree, branches break) of total *goesdownthedrain*
dedication, of playing your role
pissed, (lightning strikes nearby, temporary blindness)
you deserve *unrequitedunapologeticundying*
more *yeswhynot* (tree catches fire, sirens).

Walk Through Warsaw

We arrived in Warsaw by bus, relieved to be at
our destination after half a day of cramped legs
and recycled air. We left from Krakow, taking
the long way, the bus stopping at old cities that
were seamed together, a cloth of ancient
architecture spared from the war and the
remnants of failed communism. We spent the
night in one of the cement-block rooms the
Soviets deemed as a four-person family
apartment. You were rightly upset, for I had
spent your birthday hungover in the bus
complaining about the headache I sustained
from the sweet vodka we drank at the gay bar –
a taboo in this papal country only a decade past
– and how I was unprepared with a gift or
gratitude for your being. In Warsaw, we walked
through the plaza as tourists are wont to do:
oblivious to the surroundings we ogle at,
frantically walking into the way of established
patterns, and committing a series of serious faux
pas. I couldn't remember how many times I've
walked past the statue of the mermaid
triumphantly holding her gladius and shield, the
defendant of the city, but this was your first time
in a different continent, a novice in travel and

the humdrum of long distance. The old city
center was reborn as a relic, pointedly redone by
the inhabitants of this country asserting that, no
matter the destruction, no matter of the
innumerable lives lost in needless war, here in
the cross roads of East and West Europe, the
people of this nation still existed, that they still
persisted, resilient to total destruction like
cardinal red poppies growing in fallow fields.
For half a century, the progress of rebuilding the
city was delayed by the same repression that
destroyed it, the only difference being the
enactors. The cathedrals, the cafes, the
restaurants and ice cream parlors, businesses
housed within the brick buildings that were left
in ruins, even the sidewalks, were all turned to
rubble and ash. But, as we strolled, the ice cream
melted, trickled past the sugar cones and onto
the back of our hands. The city was full of life,
but, in the outskirts of the old town, was a half
torn down, red brick wall left from the original
castle walls. On it, a plaque rests that describes
the nothingness that once overcame the city, of
artillery that left it nearly terminal, and the fact
that all its inhabitants, even the children, took up
futile arms for its protection. Yet, I found it
difficult it was to explain why I was so reserved,
so inward reading of the people who were
almost certainly family, the generational impacts

that led my parents to abandon their homeland, the guilt I felt whenever I visit my cousins in their brutalists, concrete apartment that was smaller than a living room. Guilt covered my head and hands and toes but left the rest exposed. We walked silently out of the center. My head low. My feet dragged. My hands tucked into my armpits. When we got back to the bus stop, that's when the quarrelling began, and where I knew you couldn't understand.

Prayer; or, Mother's Appeal

God Bless Her,
She stood servile as the pitter-patter of the pestering
        faucet flaunted obscenities.
Let her have the hope her heart heaves.
Let any doubts that daunts a determined mother
disintegrate,
        the desires she degraded to a reserved reverie,
        her concerns clandestine, constrained to a corner
        of thoughts too frightening for her family.
To her, America is the eagle eager to efface her children.
So let her worries wane in whitewash runoff.
Let her have tentative tranquility.
Give her the gilded slumbers her God grants,
        and eternal peace she prays for me.
        A(woe)men.

The Hole

1.
i thought i saw you today
somewhere amidst
a faceless mass
yours stood out
in its unfamiliarity
for a brief moment
lethargic childhood nostalgia
memories alluding
so far gone
their veracity
no longer discernible

as when a mouse first feels
the stickiness underneath
and discomposure wanes
to idle acceptance
sinking into motionlessness

for that brief moment
i studied the contours
of the stranger's face
the lines demarcating age
experience, trauma

he walked away
like you
too soon
into the past

2.
darkness leaves days black
blank as thought only leads
back to remembrance of brighter times
perpetrating the cycle

this is me trapping myself
            in the hole I've created,

this is me failing to get the image
of you out of my head

this is me an idling being unmoving
            waiting fretfully for the time
            when this is but a reflection

this is me losing track of the days
weeks getting lost in the hitherto

and this is you in my room
            at your best
            an apparition

3.

day begins before dawn
during exhausted mornings
the darkness only permitting
a light grey to illuminate
our old home
as the sleet and snow
commences to cover life
and there's talk that
we'll have to delay
the end of mourning
indefinitely
until we can put to rest
the forces out of our control

Convenient, Unrequited Devotion

The signs were there:
blonde hair on her brush,
disengaging whenever touched,
irritable moods when coming home late.

But leaving is life-break
when love and convenience collude,
and even with the sentimental vicissitude
where could she go without her?

They've built their home together,
their nest full of comfort,
and she still relied on her support
even when they hardly spoke.

No, she will not poke
the hive, will not press
the issue, and emotions she'll repress
for being alone is worse than being tethered.

Recidivism

Cocooned
in temporary self-exile
awaiting for growth
to no longer hurt,
when angst subsidizes
every emotion,
when sentience blossoms
only to be stifled by
incomprehensible reality,
and there are still
years
left before
access to agency,
the youth are
convicted
for the same
nebulous crimes
of questioning, rebelling
that their parents
committed.

Human #4,234,536,345

I.
His long blackened hair drooped over his right eye,
seeing the same way he listened,
retreating from his senses as to not overload them.

Generally, the uncovered eye was underlined,
matching a turgid, darkened one
and a bruised cheek or lip.

He came to school on the same short bus
as everyone else in his neighborhood,
though he was the one who was reminded.

The dark scruff on his chin
implied his physical age,
but his mentality is on
pause, play, rewind, repeat.

He kept himself to himself,
sitting with strangers when circumstance stipulated,
getting his exercise as he rushed
from the bus back
to lock his bedroom door.

Everyone heard the yelling:
the clashing of household items,
the cacophony of discordant voices,
an attempt to subjugate differences,

and the failure of locking himself from it.

In his own world, he was evanescent –
the fly on the wall that wished to be ignored,
if only for it's humming.

He was just another son in line,
waiting his turn to get off the bus,
never forgetting how to remember,
and learning how to forget.

II.
The yelling finally stopped
(were the rumors really true?)
almost seeming like peace
bellowing from the little corner house,
and the children who lived there
came in and out
but when the oldest never did,
(were the rumors really true?)
school almost forgot him,
thinking he might have just gave up be-
cause he was always such a soft boy
(were the rumors really true?).

III.
The navy jackets carried the limp frame.

Palms clamped into red, flowing fists.

Red sprinkled over snow-spotted ground.

Screams echoed off the houses.

Blades of ochre grass punctured falling, red droplets.

Red and blue lights flashed over a blue and white car.

Audible adrenaline howled.

His face drained to pallid.

Tires screeched.

Then, silence, stillness.

IV.
It was grey the day we buried him.

Traditionally,
Catholic ceremonies
aren't held for this
type of
outcome.

However, the priest
made an exception.

The people who came stood in silence.

There were the customary speeches,
and a few people who spoke stated
they didn't know what to say,

The parents stood blank-faced, unflinching,
and there were a few nods.
By the end there was
a general agreement:
it certainly was
a tragedy.

Funambulism

Suspended on the slackline,
the world below giving way
to the undulation of change,
balancing in stupendous feat
of mental gymnastics,
you listen to NPR's
reporting on this year's
climate summit and conclude
they're fooling themselves.
idling in a parking lot,
black rubber on burning asphalt,
finding the only cool refuge
in yet another record-breaking
heat wave.

Poem Written after Following a Truck with a Bumper Sticker Insisting That I Pry It from Their Cold, Dead Hands (aka A Dark Satire)

Quiet thoughts can make the loudest bangs.
Now, agents of war have become portents of peace.
Threshold broken, why not join the parade?
Mortality is a statistic we all must face.

Why doesn't the 2nd amendment come before the 1st?
And who say you can't stuff Pandora's box?
Threshold broken, why not join the parade?
Frankly, fear is only as justified as force.

Power is a function of caliber – the endemic equalizer.
It's fifty percent off for first-time owners, no ID needed.
Now, agents of war have become portents of peace.
So why doesn't the 2nd amendment come before the 1st?

Frankly, fear is only as justified as force.
Bitch had it coming squealing like that.
It's fifty percent off for first time owners, no ID needed.
Power is a function of caliber – the endemic equalizer.

And who says you can't stuff Pandora's box?
Bitch had it coming squealing like that.
Mortality is a statistic we all must face.
Quiet thoughts can make the loudest bangs.

Because People Want Poems About Love

People want poems about love.

They want to know how your long brown hair
feels in my fingers, like silk thread flowing
soothingly healing callouses,
a holistic ending of our day to that that needs
no denouement, no climax,
just the ordinary seeming extraordinary.

They don't need to know my response
to your claim of greying strands,
and my usual retort of how I can't see
the slow progress of decaying time, or the fact that
grey is the natural color of a long held love,
the shade aging alongside
a life lived together and blends
into color-blind memories.

They don't want to know about the hair
that falls out as you brush it in the shower,
the follicle-mosaic you paint on the wall
to not clog the drain,
the agreement to disagree
of my own, natural male-pattern balding
and my fears of following in the footsteps
of my father's hairline.

Because people want poems about love,
not the quasi-philosophical conversations
of how our little dog's misbehavior
is a ramification of us not being around
because she's a saint at doggy day care,
where she's proactive, she yearns for canine
partnership in the way that new couples
not worrying superficially about the parts
of their lives they still need to keep separate
in order for them to be their own,
but intrinsically understanding temptation,
that another pup may change our hearts,
and that the comfort of settling down
is a stronger incentive than attraction.

So what if people want poems about love?

Don't they know that it boils down
to minute self-expression, pigeon-holding the poet
into a topic so redundant, so misunderstood,
a topic that shares one side of an unflippable coin,
rolling down the hill of emotion until it
finds itself in a drain being carried away
by the mosh-posh current
of human desire?

If they want to know about our love,
they should know that, after a year
of pointless bickering, you finally purchased
that new mattress because you were tired
of the existentialism of mutual debt

with the tyranny that is endemic to opinions
and the politics of comfort
making the executive decision.
We both deserve
to spend nearly a third of our lives
on something that'll always be
temporarily new.

People want to possess poems about love,
and they can hoard their feel-good poesy in barracks
like doomsdayers trying to protect themselves
in case of that impending nuclear explosion, and once
the bomb detonates, and they realize their
shelter is insufficient, it'll rain leaflets
of heartbreak and fantasies,
of the unconditionally exceptional
and the pitifully acceptable,
of deceit, retreat, conceit, repeat,
but little else of other emotion
which bares to ask
why they wanted anything else but love?

Because people want poems about love, or,
when that's unsatisfactory,
the lack there of.

Bushy Tale

The low, thinning
bushes adjacent to
an empty parking lot
of the rest stop
provides cover before
the deer makes a break
across the busy interstate
and escapes into dwindling
wilderness, a dogged
ungulate unhindered
by man's insatiable
encroachment.

90s Home Videos

Late Christmas and a few years ago
your uncle thought it a good idea
to watch some of the home movies
he made when you were little.

He thought that since we were finally
getting Serious that this was the time
to show who you were as a kid, to show
a different, younger person that looked like you.

He rummaged through the cardboard box,
wiped the dust off the cassette and
struggled to find the VHS slot
only to remember it, too, was in storage.

I helped him in rearranging the inputs,
to clean behind the TV and pick-up
the dog toys that were given up long ago as lost,
and soon, in fuzzy, VCR warmth, there you were.

You were playing catch with your cousins
in the backyard that looked unfamiliar
without snow, and the ball was thrown
over the head of the cousin I'll never meet.

"It was an accident – " you spoke faintly
as if saying the words cause it to happen again,
" – the doctor messed up the procedure,
like, it was supposed to be routine."

We watched the whole tape,

the whole family barbecue, the whole time your parents
were still together, your aunt still living in New England,
your life before schism.

But as the tape rolled, as the past revealed itself,
and the clear, early signs of your parents' troubles,
you and your cousins catching and throwing, catching and
throwing,
you curled up next to me and sobbed silently.

When it ended, when I got up and helped
clean before going to bed,
you stared blankly at grey pixilation,
at your previous life trapped in the past.

A Tour Guide to the Crumbles

1. Sint Maarten

There's a smudge on the marble countertop, she notes, as she pours herself a cup of coffee, remembering how bothersome it was to try and find a bag while grocery shopping. The price was outrageous, and she had to drive across town after the first two stores ran out of stock. Finally, she found her specific brand. Her neighbor has complained that she hasn't been able to find some for weeks, resorting to the store brand stuff for her caffeine. Gross.

Her phone buzzes. Checking the notification, she flicks the weather app's banner to the right. Fuck. The island is directly in the path of Hurricane Martha, and only two weeks after Irma! Her vacation is now certainly ruined.

She pours sugar in her coffee and mixes it with her spoon. Liquid pours over the side. Oh well. She'll just have to cancel. Maybe she can get a refund if she strongly demands it from the hotel.

Clicking the top button on her phone, she notices
the spilled coffee puddled over the smudge. She
walks towards her porch that overlooks the
valley. Her house rests high on the hill. She
remembers that it's Tuesday, and the cleaning
ladies will be here later. They can deal with the
spill later.

2. Venice

High tide,
they walk
through
shin-deep
sea water
to get to
their reservation
at the cafe,
their plastic
galoshes
wrapped
knee-height
persevering
through the
inconvenience
to have an
afternoon glass
of wine in

St. Mark's Square.

3. Portland

Huddled around the air purifier
in their living room
they pass the gas mask around
(the reverse blunt, the son joked
at first)
to get their share
of clean air
the smog obstructing visual
acuity to mere feet in front
of them and similar coughs
already developing familially
not knowing when
the fires
surrounding their
suburban home
will end.

4. NOLA

pity to those who don't love a wall
the levee built to protect the city under it
and when tide spills to waist-deep calamity

the neighborhoods afflicted were those
sanctioned
to be sacrificed pre-determinedly unsalvageable
marginalized by color on maps and faces
but she was one of the lucky ones to have to
leave
her home indefinitely with faintest of hopes to
return
to play on her favorite swing set again with her
friends
and move to that foreign land with distant
relatives
a new country of northwestern virginia

5. Polish-Belarusian Border

crossing desert and a plane flight to make the
same trek on wintery plains home destroyed
family separated they find themselves ushered at
gun point towards a line in a sand by people in
balaclavas and military gear where people yell
back in an indecipherable language and though
they're physically here hanging in legal
no-man's-land the world has reached a verdict in
abstentia

Late Pick-up

Always the last ones
          to be picked up,
always the leer
oscillated from the doorway
to us, despising us in only
the way women
looking out for other than own
can distrust youth;
no longer able to strike
the ones with
vigor,
those wild kids
with too much energy
bouncing off the walls
like wild animals
escaped from captivity;
yet too young to walk home
in a world too cold and dark
for children anymore,
yearning for when growing old enough
to be of the vulgar –
just another street kid
that police keep
both eyes on as ride bikes
outside the 7/11,

the reactive authority too immature
to remember youth and youthfulness –
to be tucked behind
dark shades, playing too cacophonously
to be effective hiders,
the seekers exhausting them
too much by running around them,
caring too little about them,
only that most early deaths
come from unneeded stress,
and the additional schoolwork
kept us occupied –
a prescription to those
grey afternoons fading into early
darkness of winter, the mid-school
drag – the seldom occasions
the clock was in double digits
when you arrived
and the guardian remonstrated that
you can't just leave them here
all night – them, a pejorative –
that we're not their responsibility,
that they don't want to hear
about the traffic.

Each time, you apologized,
which made them detest
you more, and your accent
was a nonnative slight on their lives,

acting as if no quarter should be
given to someone who doesn't speak
like them, doesn't think like they do,
for you even changed your 9 to 5
to 7:30 to 4 just so
maybe,
          just maybe,
you'd miss rush hour
in it's slowing beat
from the heart of everything
that made our and their existence possible,
the City,
and the people who occupied the menial,
and have time to pick us up
between your other employment
comprising your night
and still be late.

At least the other job
was in town, and I wondered
how many times they thought
it strange that a different
uncle or aunt picked us up
throughout the year – we had no real family
this side of the pond –
but Polaks were plentiful,
had a sense of unity,
a community
so far away from their Motherland,

and even back then as long as we
claimed we knew them we'd be
let go, setting themselves free,
for they didn't have the patience to argue,
didn't want to start a fuss,
and the one time they said no,
decided to stand up to what
they thought was right
it ended to their chagrin,
for you didn't get here until we
were already asleep
in our assigned seats,
our heads resting on the table,
and your received reprimand
woke us up.

We've left, all of us, grown up,
but habits, even out of necessity,
die hard, tend to
rub off, your schedule
hasn't altered.

Last time I called
we talked about work,
saying
today will be a long day.
yesterday was long, too,
and tomorrow
looks much the same,

and when will it change?

Who knows?

Done Time

The doorbell rings, but he can barely hear it over
the TV (time is all he has) when the second knock
occurs, that's when he notices the blurry screen
and recognizes there's someone out there, and with
cracking knees, creaking boards, arthritic hands
he manages to turn the knob, opens to see
a young man – a boy really – who asks
if this is the right address, if he'd
requested someone to help fix his internet,
and he stammers a bit, rubs his hands over the
bald, brown-spotted scalp, sees the him in him, tries
to relate, to express, but lets him in,
sits on the couch, and forgets about him.

Homage to Health

The bill finally came in the mail.

The page had been elongated for sufficient
space.

Fold after fold fell towards the ground.

They read the list, individually screening the
lines.

The left margin held audacious robbery.

The right margin deducted salvation.

What's certain was they needed this job.

It floated over their heads like dark clouds.

The storm hadn't broken just yet, but shelter was
nowhere near.

Heads spun worse than what had brought them
to this point.

They prayed for good health.

It went unanswered.

Doctor said they were lucky to find it early.

Pills won't be covered fully, though.

Each week brought refill and withdrawal.

They kept working, life consolidated, coerced.

Existence barely beat bankruptcy.

The days wore on.

Time crumbled.

They continued to survive until they couldn't.

No one's last thoughts need to be about debt.

The Release of an Inmate as a
Different Person

Wearing the only suit he's known,
pants snug around his now thickened waist,

his body filled with time and processed food,
the minimal nutrients permanently blanching
complexion,

the sunlight that passed the gate seemed
so much brighter, more omnipresent

than that penetrating into the cells,
and infiltration rather than welcomed

necessity, cold illumination other
than bright, commonplace warmth,

and there his brother chuckles
that peters out slowly, the lack

of a maternal figure felt, now dead
during the long years, as his missing presence

was felt during the procession,
the specter standing alone in the back,

too far away to be able to have said goodbye
to isolated to know even much later,

and his brother teases him to brighten
the mood over what he's wearing,

him wanting to look good during
his first moments of freedom, and even

with all those years he knew things wouldn't
be the same, but how can fashion

be so different, how can culture change
so that what he did is no longer a crime,

how could he walk with his head held
high with so much of his life taken, so much

liberty, and how can not feel diffidence, be so
underserving, of being on the other side,

of the guilt compounded each year of the time
taken from him, of the missed moments,

of being
released.